A Catholic Prayer Companion

A Heartwarming Collection of 30 Best-Loved Catholic Prayers

Compiled by Gregory F. Augustine Pierce

ASSISTING CHRISTIANS TO ACT
PUBLICATIONS

A Catholic Prayer Companion
A Heartwarming Collection of 30 Best-Loved Catholic Prayers

Compiled by Gregory F. Augustine Pierce
Cover Design by Tom A. Wright
Typesetting by Desktop Edit Shop, Inc.

English translation of the *Confiteor* and the *Litany of the Saints* from *The Roman Missal* © 1973, International Committee on English in the Liturgy, Inc. (ICEL); the English translation of the *Angelus; Memorare; Salve, Regine; Regina Caeli;* and "Come, Holy Spirit" from *A Book of Prayers* © 1982, ICEL. Used with permission. All rights reserved.

English translation of the *Gloria in Excelsis, Sanctus and Benedictus, Agnus Dei, Te Deum Laudamus,* and *Magnificat* by the International Consultation on English Texts.

Published by ACTA Publications, 4848 N. Clark Street, Chicago, IL 60640 (800) 397-2282 www.actapublications.com, actapublications@aol.com

Printed in the United States of America
ISBN: 0-87946-266-3
Year 10 9 8 7 6 5 4
Printing 10 9 8 7 6 5 4 3 2 1

Contents

Introduction

Catholic tradition has an abundance of beautiful prayers:

- Prayers to God—the Father, Son and Holy Spirit;
- Prayers to Mary, the mother of Jesus;
- Prayers from the holy sacrifice of the Mass;
- Prayers to and by the saints;
- Prayers said around the home;
- Blessings of many kinds and for many occasions.

These prayers form a rich treasury that is ours, free for the taking; but many times we forget the exact words or never learn them in the first place. This *Catholic Prayer Companion* offers thirty of the best known and most loved Catholic prayers. You may pray the prayers straight through or go directly to individual prayers in whatever number and order you wish.

As Fr. Martin Pable says in his book, *Prayer: A Practical Guide:* "Traditional and formula prayers are gifts to us on our spiritual journey. When we don't know how or what to say to God—when 'words fail us'—we Catholics draw upon simple, familiar forms of prayer that we learned at our mother's knee, or during our religious education, or from the ancient words of the Bible. We possess a rich treasury indeed."

Therefore, let us begin.

*Prayers to
the Father, the Son,
and the Holy Spirit*

THE SIGN OF THE CROSS

In the name of the Father, and of the Son,
and of the Holy Spirit. Amen.

THE LORD'S PRAYER

Our Father, who art in heaven,
hallowed be thy name;
thy Kingdom come, thy will be done,
on earth as it is in heaven.

Give us this day our daily bread;
and forgive us our trespasses,
as we forgive those who trespass against us;
and lead us not into temptation,
but deliver us from evil. Amen.

THE PRAYER OF PRAISE

Glory be to the Father,
and to the Son,
and to the Holy Spirit.
As it was in the beginning,
is now and ever shall be,
world without end. Amen.

THE PRAYER TO THE HOLY SPIRIT

Come, Holy Spirit, fill my heart
   with your holy gifts.
Let my weakness be penetrated
   with your strength this very day,
that I may fulfill all the duties
   of my state conscientiously,
that I may do what is right and just.

Let my charity be such as to offend no one,
   and hurt no one's feelings;
so generous as to pardon sincerely
   any wrong done to me.

Assist me, O Holy Spirit, in all my trials of life,
   enlighten me in my ignorance,
   advise me in my doubts,
   strengthen me in my weakness,
   help me in all my needs,
   protect me in temptations,
   and console me in afflictions.

Graciously hear me, O Holy Spirit,
   and pour your light into my heart,
   my soul, and my mind.

Assist me to live a holy life,
   and to grow in goodness and grace. Amen.

THE DIVINE PRAISES

Blessed be God.
Blessed be his Holy Name.
Blessed be Jesus Christ, true God and true man.
Blessed be the name of Jesus.
Blessed be his most Sacred Heart.
Blessed be Jesus,
    in the most Holy Sacrament of the Altar.
Blessed be the Holy Spirit, the Paraclete.
Blessed be the great Mother of God,
    Mary most holy.
Blessed be her holy and Immaculate Conception.
Blessed be her glorious Assumption.
Blessed be the name of Mary, Virgin and Mother.
Blessed be St. Joseph, her most chaste spouse.
Blessed be God, in his angels and in his saints.

May the heart of Jesus,
    in the Most Blessed Sacrament,
be praised, adored, and loved
    with grateful affection,
at every moment,
    in all the tabernacles of the world,
even to the end of time. Amen.

THE PRAYER TO THE BLESSED TRINITY

The Father is my hope. The Son is my refuge.
The Holy Spirit is my protector.
Glory to the holy and undivided Trinity,
   now and for ever.

Let us praise the Father, the Son,
   and the Holy Spirit;
let us bless and exalt God above all for ever!

Almighty and everlasting God, to whom we owe
the grace of professing the true faith, grant that
while acknowledging the glory of the eternal
Trinity and adoring its unity, we may, through
your majestic power, be confirmed in this faith
and defended against all adversities; through Jesus
Christ our Lord, who lives and reigns with you,
in the unity of the Holy Spirit, one God, for ever
and ever. Amen.

THE TE DEUM

You are God: we praise you;
　You are the Lord: we acclaim you;
You are the eternal Father:
　All creation worships you.
To you all angels, all the powers of heaven,
Cherubim and Seraphim, sing in endless praise:
Holy, holy, holy Lord, God of power and might,
Heaven and earth are full of your glory.
The glorious company of apostles praise you.
The noble fellowship of prophets praise you.
The white-robed army of martyrs praise you.
Throughout the world,
　the holy Church acclaims you:
Father, of majesty unbounded;
　your true and only Son,
　worthy of all worship;
　and the Holy Spirit,
　advocate and guide.
You, Christ, are the king of glory,
　the eternal Son of the Father.
When you became man to set us free,
　you did not spurn the Virgin's womb.

(continued)

You overcame the sting of death,
and opened the kingdom of heaven
   to all believers.
You are seated at God's right hand in glory.
We believe that you will come, and be our judge.
Come then, Lord, and help your people,
bought with the price of your own blood,
and bring us with your saints to glory everlasting.
Save your people, Lord,
   and bless your inheritance.
Govern and uphold them now and always.
Day by day we bless you.
   We praise your name for ever.
Keep us today, Lord, from all sin.
   Have mercy on us, Lord, have mercy.
Lord, show us your love and mercy;
   for we put our trust in you.
In you, Lord, is our hope:
   and we shall never hope in vain. Amen.

COME, HOLY SPIRIT

V. Come, Holy Spirit,
fill the hearts of your faithful.

R. And kindle in them the fire of your love.

V. Send forth your Spirit,
and they shall be created.

R. And you shall renew the face of the earth.

Let us pray.
Lord, by the light of the Holy Spirit,
you have taught the hearts of your faithful.
In the same Spirit, help us to choose what is
right, and always rejoice in your consolation.
We ask this through Christ, our Lord. Amen.

VENI, SANCTE SPIRITUS

Come, thou Holy Spirit, come!
   And from thy celestial home
   shed a ray of light divine!
Come, thou Father of the poor!
   Come thou source of all our store!
Come, within our bosoms shine!
Thou, of comforters the best;
   Thou, the soul's most welcome guest;
   Sweet refreshment here below.
In our labor, rest most sweet:
   Grateful coolness in the heat;
   Solace in the midst of woe.
O most blessed Light divine,
   shine within these hearts of thine,
   and our inmost being fill!
Where thou art not, we have naught,
   nothing good in deed or thought,
   nothing free from taint of ill.
Heal our wounds, our strength renew;
   On our dryness pour thy dew;
   Wash the stains of guilt away.
Bend the stubborn heart and will;
   Melt the frozen, warm the chill;
   Guide the steps that go astray.
On the faithful, who adore,
   and confess thee evermore,
   in thy sev'nfold gift descend.
Give them virtue's sure reward;
   Give them thy salvation, Lord;
Give them joys that never end. Amen.

Prayers to Mary

THE HAIL MARY

Hail Mary, full of grace; the Lord is with thee;
blessed art thou amongst women,
and blessed is the fruit of thy womb, Jesus.

Holy Mary, mother of God, pray for us sinners,
now and at the hour of our death. Amen.

HAIL, HOLY QUEEN

Hail, Holy Queen, Mother of Mercy, our life,
our sweetness and our hope.
To thee do we cry, poor banished children of Eve,
to thee do we send up our sighs,
mourning and weeping in this vale of tears.

Turn, then, most gracious advocate,
thine eyes of mercy toward us;
and after this our exile,
show unto us the blessed fruit of thy womb, Jesus.

O clement, O loving, O sweet Virgin Mary.

Pray for us, O holy Mother of God,
that we may be made worthy
     of the promises of Christ.

THE MEMORARE
(attributed to St. Bernard of Clairvaux)

Remember, O most gracious Virgin Mary,
that never was it known,
that anyone who fled to your protection,
implored your help, or sought your intercession,
was left unaided.

Inspired by this confidence, I fly to you,
O Virgin of Virgins, my Mother.
To you do I come, before you I stand,
   sinful and sorrowful.

O Mother of the Word Incarnate,
   despise not my petitions,
but in your mercy hear and answer me. Amen.

THE ANGELUS

V. The angel of the Lord declared unto Mary,

R. And she conceived of the Holy Spirit.

Hail, Mary, full of grace, the Lord is with thee,
blessed art thou amongst women and blessed
is the fruit of thy womb, Jesus.
Holy Mary, Mother of God, pray for us sinners
now, and at the hour of our death. Amen.

V. "I am the handmaid of the Lord,

R. Be it done unto me according to thy word."

Hail, Mary, full of grace, the Lord is with thee,
blessed art thou amongst women and blessed
is the fruit of thy womb, Jesus.
Holy Mary, Mother of God, pray for us sinners
now, and at the hour of our death. Amen.

V. The Word became flesh,

R. And dwelt amongst us.

(continued)

*Hail, Mary, full of grace, the Lord is with thee,
blessed art thou amongst women and blessed
is the fruit of thy womb, Jesus.
Holy Mary, Mother of God, pray for us sinners
now, and at the hour of our death. Amen.*

V. Pray for us, O holy Mother of God,

R. That we may be made worthy
of the promises of Christ.

Let us pray.
Pour forth, we beseech thee, O Lord, thy
grace into our hearts, that we to whom
the incarnation of Christ, your son, was
made known by the message of an angel may
by his passion and cross be brought to the
glory of his resurrection, through the same
Christ, our Lord. Amen.

THE REGINA CAELI

V. Queen of heaven, rejoice, alleluia,

R. For Christ, your Son and Son of God,

V. Has risen as he said, alleluia.

R. Pray for us to God, alleluia.

V. Rejoice and be glad, O Virgin Mary, alleluia,

R. For the Lord has truly risen, alleluia.

Let us pray:
God of life, you have given joy to the world
by the resurrection of your Son, Our Lord Jesus
Christ. Through the prayers of his mother, the
Virgin Mary, bring us to the happiness of
eternal life. We ask this through Christ, our
Lord. Amen.

THE MAGNIFICAT

My soul magnifies the Lord,
    and my spirit rejoices in God my savior,
for he has looked with favor
    on the lowliness of his servant.

Surely, from now on all generations
    will call me blessed:
for the Mighty One has done great things for me,
    and holy is his Name.

His mercy is for those who fear him
    from generation to generation.

He has shown strength with his arm;
    he has scattered the proud
    in the thoughts of their hearts.

He has brought down the powerful
    from their thrones,
    and has lifted up the lowly.

He has filled the hungry with good things,
    and sent the rich away empty.

He has helped his servant Israel,
    in remembrance of his mercy,
    according to the promise he made
    to our ancestors, to Abraham
    and to his descendants for ever. Amen.

Prayers
from
the Mass

THE CONFITEOR

I confess to almighty God, and to you,
   my brothers and sisters,
that I have sinned, through my own fault,
   in my thoughts and in my words,
in what I have done,
   and in what I have failed to do;
and I ask blessed Mary, ever virgin,
   all the angels and saints,
and you, my brothers and sisters,
   to pray for me to the Lord our God.

THE GLORIA

Glory to God in the highest,
   and peace to his people on earth.
Lord God, heavenly King,
   almighty God and Father,
We worship you, we give you thanks,
   we praise you for your glory.
Lord Jesus Christ, only Son of the Father,
Lord God, Lamb of God,
   you take away the sin of the world:
   have mercy on us;
You are seated at the right hand of the Father:
   receive our prayer.
For you alone are the Holy One,
   you alone are the Lord,
You alone are the Most High, Jesus Christ,
   with the Holy Spirit,
In the glory of God the Father. Amen.

THE SANCTUS

Holy, holy, holy Lord, God of power and might,
Heaven and earth are full of your glory.
Hosanna in the highest.
Blessed is he who comes in the name of the Lord,
Hosanna in the highest.

THE AGNUS DEI

Lamb of God,
you take away the sin of the world:
have mercy on us.

Lamb of God,
you take away the sin of the world:
have mercy on us.

Lamb of God,
you take away the sin of the world:
grant us peace.

Prayers to and by the Saints

THE LITANY OF THE SAINTS

V. Lord, have mercy
on us

R. Lord, have mercy
on us.

V. Christ, have mercy
on us.

R. Christ, have mercy
on us.

V. Lord, have mercy
on us.

R. Lord, have mercy
on us.

V. Holy Mary, Mother
of God,

R. Pray for us.

V. St. Michael,

R. Pray for us.

V. Holy Angels of God,

R. Pray for us.

V. St. Joseph,

R. Pray for us.

V. St. John the Baptist,

R. Pray for us.

V. St. Peter and St. Paul,

R. Pray for us.

V. St. Andrew,

R. Pray for us.

V. St. John,

R. Pray for us.

V. St. Mary Magdalene,

R. Pray for us.

V. St. Stephen,

R. Pray for us.

V. St. Ignatius,

R. Pray for us.

V. St. Lawrence,

R. Pray for us.

V. St. Perpetua and
St. Felicity,

R. Pray for us.

V. St. Agnes,

R. Pray for us.

V. St. Gregory,

R. Pray for us.

V. St. Augustin,

R. Pray for us.

V. St. Athanasius,

R. Pray for us.

V. St. Basil,

R. Pray for us.

V. St. Martin,

R. Pray for us.

V. St. Benedict,

R. Pray for us.

(continued)

V. St. Francis and
St. Dominic, **R.** Pray for us.
V. St. Francis Xavier, **R.** Pray for us.
V. St. John Vianney, **R.** Pray for us.
V. St. Catherine, **R.** Pray for us.
V. All you saints of God, **R.** Pray for us.

V. Lord, be merciful, **R.** Lord, save us.
V. From all harm, **R.** Lord, save us.
V. From every sin, **R.** Lord, save us.
V. From all temptations, **R.** Lord, save us.
V. From everlasting
death, **R.** Lord, save us.
V. By your coming
among us, **R.** Lord, save us.
V. By your death and
rising to a new life, **R.** Lord, save us.
V. By your gift of the
Holy Spirit, **R.** Lord, save us.

V. Be merciful to us
sinners, **R.** Lord, hear our prayer.
V. Guide and protect
your Holy Church, **R.** Lord, hear our prayer.
V. Keep our Pope and all
the clergy in faithful
service to your Church, **R.** Lord, hear our prayer.
V. Bring all people together
in trust and peace, **R.** Lord, hear our prayer.
V. Strengthen us in your
service, **R.** Lord, hear our prayer.

THE PRAYER OF ST. IGNATIUS LOYOLA

Soul of Christ, be my sanctification;
    Body of Christ, be my salvation;
Blood of Christ, fill all my veins;
    Water from Christ's side,
    wash out my stains;
Passion of Christ, my comfort be;
    O good Jesus, listen to me:
In thy wounds I fain would hide,
    ne'er to be parted from thy side;
Guard me, should the foe assail me;
    Call me when my life shall fail me;
Bid me come to thee above,
    with thy saints to sing thy love,
World without end. Amen.

THE PRAYER OF ST. TERESA OF AVILA

Majestic Sovereign, timeless wisdom,
Your kindness melts my hard, cold soul.
Handsome lover, selfless giver,
Your beauty fills my dull, sad eyes.

I am yours, you made me.
I am yours, you called me.
I am yours, you saved me.
I am yours, you loved me.
I will never leave your presence.

Give me death, give me life.
Give me sickness, give me health.
Give me honor, give me shame.
Give me weakness, give me strength.
I will have whatever you give. Amen.

THE PRAYER OF ST. FRANCIS

Lord, make me an instrument of your peace.
Where there is hatred, let me sow love;
Where there is injury, pardon;
   where there is doubt, faith;
Where there is despair, hope;
   where there is darkness, light;
And where there is sadness, joy.

O Divine Master,
   grant that I may not so much
   seek to be consoled as to console;
   to be understood as to understand;
   to be loved as to love;
For it is in giving that we receive;
   and it is in dying
   that we are born to eternal life. Amen.

THE BREASTPLATE OF ST. PATRICK

Christ with me, Christ before me,
   Christ behind me, Christ in me,
Christ beneath me, Christ above me,
   Christ on my right, Christ on my left,
Christ in breadth, Christ in length,
   Christ in height,
Christ in the mouth of everyone
   who speaks to me,
Christ in the heart of everyone
   who thinks of me,
Christ in every eye that sees me,
   Christ in every ear that hears me.

I arise today
Through a mighty strength,
   the invocation of the Trinity,
Through belief in the Threeness,
Through confession of the Oneness,
Of the Creator of Creation. Amen.

Prayers around the Home

THE ACT OF CONTRITION

O my God, I am heartily sorry for having offended you, and I detest all my sins, because of your just punishments, but most of all because they offend you, my God, who are all good and deserving of all my love. I firmly resolve, with the help of your grace, to sin no more and to avoid the near occasion of sin. Amen.

THE MORNING OFFERING

O Jesus, through the Immaculate Heart of Mary, I offer you all my prayers, works, joys, and sufferings of this day, for all the intentions of your Sacred Heart, in union with the holy sacrifice of the Mass throughout the world, in reparation for my sins, for the intentions of all our associates, and for the general intention recommended this month. Amen.

GRACE BEFORE MEALS

Bless us, O Lord, and these thy gifts,
   which we are about to receive,
from thy bounty,
   through Christ Our Lord. Amen.

PRAYER TO OUR GUARDIAN ANGEL

Angel of God, my Guardian Dear, to whom God's love commits me here, ever this day be at my side, to light and guard, to rule and guide. Amen.

Blessings

THE HERITAGE BLESSING

May the God of Abraham, Isaac, and Jacob,
May the God of Peter, James, and John,
May the God of us all, bless us
In the name of the Father, Son, and Holy Spirit.
Amen.

AN IRISH BLESSING

May the road rise to meet you,
May the wind be always at your back,
May the sun shine warm upon your face,
May the rains fall soft upon your fields.
And until we meet again,
May God hold you in the palm of his hand.
Amen.

PRAYER FOR THOSE WHO HAVE DIED

May the souls of the faithful departed,
    through the mercy of God, rest in peace. Amen.

Eternal rest grant unto them, O Lord,
    and let perpetual light shine upon them. Amen.

May they rest in peace. Amen.